The Ultimate Self-Teaching Method!

Level 1

Play Dobro Today!

A Complete Guide to the Basics

T0085387

To access audio visit:
www.halleonard.com/mylibrary

Enter Code
1913-0901-0094-2764

by Stacy Phillips

Edited by Chad Johnson

ISBN 978-1-4234-9162-0

HAL•LEONARD®
CORPORATION

7777 W. BLUEMOUND RD. P.O. BOX 13819 M LWAUKEE, WI 53213

In Australia Contact:
Hal Leonard Australia Pty. Ltd.
4 Lentara Court
Cheltenham, Victoria, 3192 Australia
Email: ausadmin@halleonard.com.au

Visit Hal Leonard Online at
www.halleonard.com

Introduction

Track 1

Welcome to *Play Dobro Today!* and the wondrous world of Dobro playing. This book will get you picking, sliding, and rolling right from the first time you put on picks. Each lesson builds on the previous ones, so try to have a handle on the material before moving ahead. Don't be satisfied with out-of-tune and out-of-time playing. For practice purposes, play all the music as slowly as necessary to be correct. Absolute perfection may not be necessary, but have confidence that your playing has improved before starting the next lesson.

About the Audio

For instant access to the audio examples that accompany this book, simply go to www.halleonard.com/mylibrary and enter the code found on page 1.

It is very helpful to have a device or computer software that can change the tempo of the audio without changing its pitch; this way, you can practice at whatever pace is comfortable and have a way to gauge progress. When a track on the recording features a melody, the stereo channels are separated into melody and rhythm so that you can play along with, isolate, or blend the channels.

About the Author

Stacy Phillips is a Grammy award-winning Dobro player and violinist. He has performed on four continents with many of the finest acoustic musicians in the world. He is the author of over 25 acclaimed books and DVDs on various aspects of his chosen instruments. Check out his website at *www.stacy-phillips.com.*

Contents

Lesson 1 | Basics

The term "Dobro" is a trademark that usually refers to a specific design of slide guitar, its inventor's family, "**Do**pjera **Bro**thers," and is also a pun on the term for "good" in their native Slovakian, "*dobra*." The original Dobro was designed to be a loud acoustic instrument in the days before electric guitars, amplifiers, and effective sound reinforcement. This involves raised strings and a square neck to help withstand the added pressure resulting from raised strings.

Nomenclature for this instrument is a bit loose. "Steel guitar" (or just "steel"), "lap guitar," "lap slide," and "Hawaiian guitar" generally refer to the same instrument: any guitar played flat on its back. "Dobro," "resonator," or "resophonic guitar" relate to that instrument with a ***resonator*** placed inside the body. (This thin, aluminum, usually concave plate is attached to the strings via the bridge and creates a complex timbre, full of rich overtones.)

This book teaches fundamental techniques applicable to all the above. While there are 8- and even 10-string models, I refer to the most popular 6-string version, using **high bass G tuning**.

The ***bar*** (sometimes also called "steel") refers to the metal implement that touches the strings. It is also used as a verb, indicating the "act of putting the metal to the strings." (Do not use the hollow plastic tubes favored by bottleneck guitarists. Their light weight results in relatively poor tone on a Dobro.) If you are going to play bluegrass, look for a bar with a sharp edge to ease pull-offs (modeled after the long-time sole manufacturer of that design, Stevens bar); otherwise, bullet bars are favored.

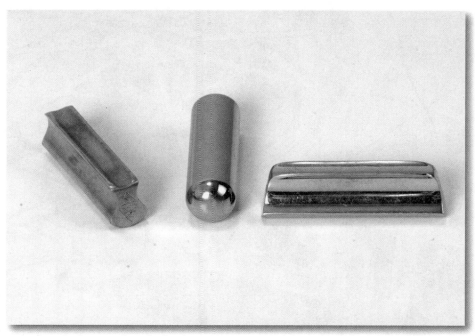

L to R: Stevens bar, bullet bar, Stevens-style bar with angled nose that facilitates pull-offs

Dobro Anatomy

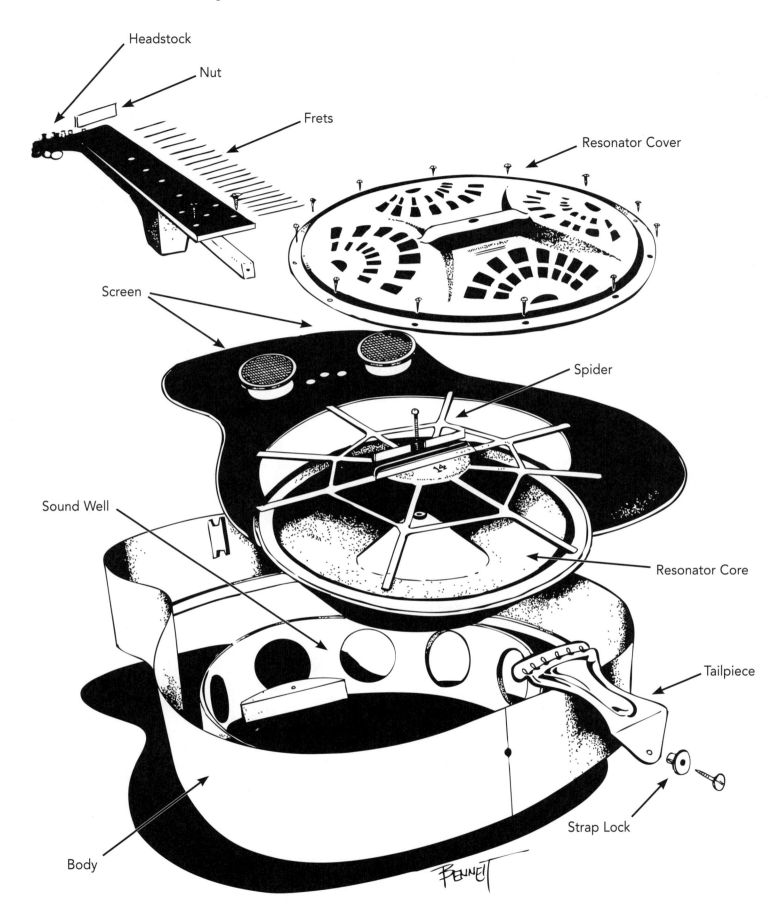

Headstock

Nut

Frets

Resonator Cover

Screen

Spider

Sound Well

Resonator Core

Tailpiece

Strap Lock

Body

BENNETT

Holding Your Dobro

Track 2

► The small jack is for attaching and plugging in a microphone. The socket under the strap is for a stereo cable for both the microphone and pickup.

Attachment of strap on the side of the body.

When playing Dobro, it is highly recommended that you use a strap. There are commercially made straps designed for the specifications of acoustic lap-style guitars. If local stores do not stock them (likely), it is best to search the internet. At present, there are several Dobro discussion groups that have tons of information about such matters in their archives.

There is a button on the side of the Dobro's body that attaches to one end of the strap. The other end winds around the **headstock** in the space between the second and third strings on the side of the headstock farthest from you, and fourth and fifth strings on the other. See the photos for a clearer depiction.

Placement of strap on headstock.

Standing

Standing posture showing right arm wrapped around the strap. Spreading your legs eases strain on your neck and back.

When standing, it is recommended that you wrap your picking arm around the strap, as illustrated in the accompanying photos. This transfers some of the Dobro's weight from your neck to the shoulder. This stance also makes the Dobro a bit more stable when you stand. Make certain that the strap does not exert upwards pressure on your fourth or fifth string tuning pegs.

Most people wear the strap so the Dobro's body is situated near the waist when you are standing. As a matter of comfort, you don't want to have to lift your arms much to reach the strings. Try to place the Dobro's body in the same area of the waist when seated and standing so that your arms and hands are in the same position either way.

Sitting

While sitting, placing the body on one leg and neck on the other stabilizes the Dobro. I like having the body tilted a bit towards me.

Playing while seated is definitely easier for beginners because the lap provides stability for the Dobro. Get some of the basics down before experimenting with playing while standing. I usually do not use the strap while seated, but some Dobro players like the added security.

Picks

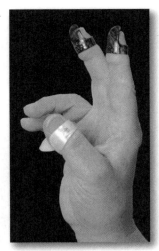

▶ Fingerpicks are curled around the fingertips. There are no right angles. There are players who have the picks standing almost straight out and others who curl them even more than in this photo.

Most people use a thumb-pick and metal fingerpicks. You should experiment with some of the many designs and thicknesses that are commercially available until you find the type that is the most comfortable and delivers the best tone for you.

Metal fingerpicks are especially easy to bend and shape to your fingers. How much they curve around your fingertips as opposed to sticking straight up is a matter of taste and how your fingers work. Plastic picks require sitting for a few moments in very hot water (not too long!), which softens them a bit. When soft, put them on and shape to your finger. Another variable is how tightly they fit—tight enough to not slip, but not too tight to cut off blood circulation!

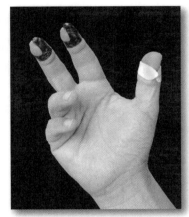

Thumb-pick and fingerpicks offset so they hit the strings straight on.

Some folks like to rest their pinky and/or bottom of the palm against the cover plate. This is one of many issues that is not a matter of right or wrong, but of comfort. Note that, when my hand is comfortable, my fingers are ready to strike the strings at a slight angle (i.e., not perpendicular to the strings). I angle my fingerpicks a bit to take this into account, enabling the picks to hit the strings at 90 degrees. Some players are comfortable twisting their wrist a bit so the fingers hit perpendicularly.

Typical right-hand picking posture with offset fingerpicks.

Alternate approach while wearing straightened fingerpicks.

Track 3

Tuning Up

Do *not* use strings that are gauged for standard guitar. D'Addario Phosphor Bronze J-42 sets are probably the current industry standard for Dobros, but again, experiment.

Try to match your strings to the pitches on the audio by gradually and carefully turning the corresponding tuning pegs on the headstock. Here are a few things to be aware of that will ease the process:

- It is easier to tune up from a string that is flat than to tune down from one that is sharp—take your time.
- Pick the string just before you turn the tuning peg so that you can hear just how much you are changing the pitch. This will help ensure that a string is not tuned too high, causing it to break (a bad thing).
- Your string will sound dissonant to the pitches on the track when it gets very close to being in tune. When the track and your string are in tune, it will suddenly sound like one loud note.

Depending on how much you play, the strings will eventually become more difficult to tune as they age and may start to buzz as their wrapping eventually loosens. Then it will be time to replace the old ones.

Starting with the lowest, fattest string (the one closest to your body when you are in playing position), the Dobro is tuned to the pitches: G–B–D–G–B–D. The last D is the highest-pitched, thinnest string (the one farthest from your body when in playing position).

Track 4

Tuning Notes

The G, B, and D notes (played in any order) create a G major chord when sounded simultaneously. By just strumming the open strings you're already playing one of the most popular chords you will need in the future!

Track 5

Using a Keyboard

If the accompanying recording is not handy, you can also tune by matching pitches with a different instrument. Keyboards are fairly ubiquitous these days, and the electronic ones stay in tune. Use your ear to match pitches, remembering to tune the strings up.

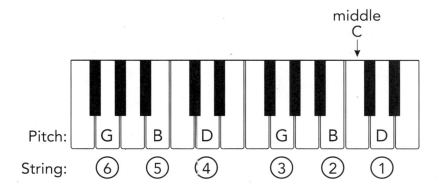

Using an Electronic Tuner

There are some small but effective electronic tuners that are light enough to clip onto the head-stock. Their readouts allow you to see whether your string is pitched too high or low. These gadgets are especially useful when it's noisy where you are trying to tune. However, after using any electronic tuner, you still have to fine-tune with your ears.

Relative Tuning

If you can reliably tune one string from another instrument, like a piano or pitch pipe, you can use it to tune the rest. The first string (D note) is the easiest one to use as a start. Then:

1. Tune the second string, third fret to match the open first string.

2. Then tune the third string, fourth fret to match the open second string.

3. Then tune the fourth string, fifth fret to match the open third.

4. Tune the fifth string, third fret to match the open fourth.

5. Tune the sixth string, fourth fret to match the open fifth.

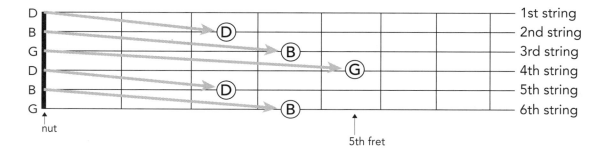

Reading Music for the Dobro

Music for the Dobro is commonly notated in two ways: **standard notation** and **tablature**. In this book, we'll use both.

Standard Notation

Pitch

Standard music notation employs a five-line **staff**. Circular **noteheads** are placed either on the lines or in the spaces between.

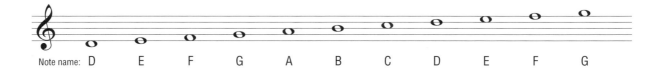

Note name: D   E   F   G   A   B   C   D   E   F   G

This symbol (𝄞) is called the **treble clef** and indicates that the music is using the pitch definitions of the lines and spaces just illustrated.

There are several pieces in the book that have higher pitches than those above the staff—**ledger lines** are used above or below the staff to indicate these. It can be difficult to read very high notes in standard notation. In context, it will be easy with the help of tablature.

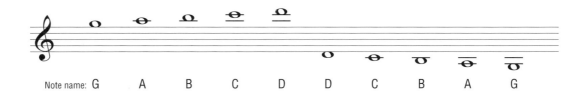

Note name: G   A   B   C   D   D   C   B   A   G

Rhythm

The term **rhythm** refers to the speed and duration of the notes we play. Rhythms are indicated with different symbols:

Whole Note   Half Note   Quarter Note
(4 beats)   (2 beats)   (1 beat)

Music is separated into **measures** (or **bars**) by **bar lines**, making it easier to keep your place. The **time signature** (or "meter") at the beginning of each piece tells you the beat structure. The top number tells you how many beats are in a measure. The bottom number indicates which note value is counted as one beat. In 4/4 (the most common meter), there are four beats per measure, and the quarter note is counted as the beat.

Tablature

Tablature for Dobro uses a six-line staff, with each line representing one of the Dobro's strings. Remember that all the examples in this book are in high bass G tuning, from low to high: G–B–D–G–B–D.

Pitch

Each of the tablature's six lines represents a string, with the thinnest, highest-pitched string (D) at the top of the staff and the thickest, lowest-pitched string (G) at the bottom. This is just like looking down at your Dobro in playing position with the thickest string closest to your body. A number on a line indicates the fret and string that should be played.

So the next example means that you should pick the first string at the third fret, the open first string, the second string at fret 10, and finally, strings 1 and 2 simultaneously at fret 8.

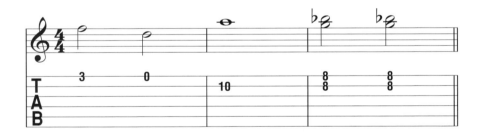

Three or more numbers in a column of the tablature staff are typically performed by a strum (see "Lesson 6—Chord Accompaniment") with the thumbpick. The following indicates an open-string strum of all six strings.

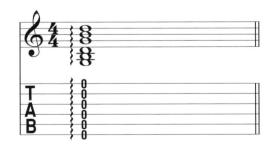

Slurs and Glisses (Slides)

One of the signature sounds of the Dobro guitar is the sound of pitches sliding up or down to one another. This technique is called a **gliss** or **slide**, and it's achieved by touching the bar to a string, plucking the string, and moving the bar up or down its length while maintaining contact. This is indicated in the notation by a slanted line connecting two pitches.

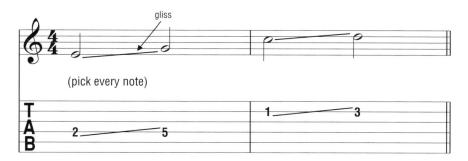

If you also see an arced line, called a **slur**, connecting the pitches, this tells you to not pick the second (destination) note.

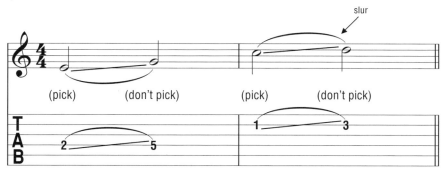

Diagonal lines attached to only one note refer to (usually quick) slides of indeterminate length (usually one or two frets). The direction of the lines indicate the direction of the slide. The first slide is "up to," and the next is "down from."

Other Symbols

When a specific pick-hand fingering is recommended, it is placed just above the tablature staff.

"T" is thumb, "I" is index finger, and "M" is middle finger. Capital letters above the tablature indicate the chordal accompaniment.

Neck Diagrams

Another way of indicating notes, scales, or chords on the Dobro (or any fretted instrument) is with a **neck diagram** (or **chord grid**). This is a vertical representation of a portion of the guitar's neck, viewed as if the instrument was hanging on the wall in front of you. The six vertical lines represent the six strings—the lowest pitched (thickest) being on the left and the highest pitched (thinnest) on the right. The horizontal lines represent the frets.

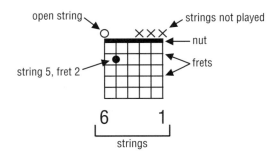

When a diagram represents a portion of the neck that's not in open position, a fret marker will indicate the position. In the following grid, the first fret shown is the seventh fret.

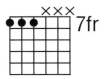

Grids can also be placed horizontally, which are viewed as you see the neck while in playing position. In this type of grid, the horizontal lines represent the strings—thickest on bottom—and the vertical lines represent the frets. These are generally used most often to demonstrate scale shapes. Again, if the grid shows a portion of the neck other than open position, a fret marker will indicate the position.

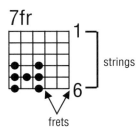

That's a lot of yakking. Let's grab our Dobros and get ready to make some noise!

Basic Bar Control

Track 9

Most of the time you don't really "hold" the bar. The weight of the bar, along with the index finger resting (*not* pressing down) on top of it, creates sufficient pressure for a pleasing tone. Only when the bar is not touching the strings (i.e., when picking open strings or moving from one fret to another *without* slides) is it truly held.

To get the idea, place your hand (without the bar) on the strings in a completely relaxed manner. The only pressure on the strings should be from the weight of your hand. Let it relax and sag a bit.

► Note the index and middle fingers extending past the bar and also the middle finger, index finger, and pinky lying on the strings.

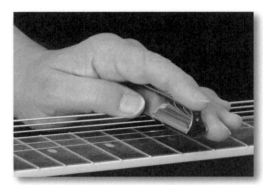

Keeping that same free-from-tension approach, slip the bar under your index finger. It should be far enough into the palm that the index and middle fingers extend past the bar. How much past? Place the bar so that it covers the lowest five strings at any fret. The overlapping index and middle fingers should be able to touch the first string (the one not covered by the bar). It is not necessarily a bad sign if you occasionally drop the bar at this stage. If any part of your hand or arm aches after a practice session, take heed! You are probably grabbing too tightly at least part of the time. An occasional drop indicates that you are not.

Damping (Blocking)

The fingers behind the bar (the ones closer to the nut) should remain on the strings in a relaxed manner. I will refer to those as the "damping fingers." These fingers help to avoid unwanted noise caused by the bar rattling against the strings, which is known as "bar chatter."

Before launching into a melody, let's practice this critical damping technique (also called **blocking**) with some chording. This exercise has three chords: G, C, and D. Use your thumb to strum the strings.

The first chord, G, is played without the bar. The muting fingers behind the bar should touch the strings a split second before strumming the C chord at fret 5. When the fingers touch, quickly rotate your wrist the small amount necessary to place the bar on the strings.

► When playing open strings, hover as close to the strings as possible to minimize motion.

For bar-control practice, don't use any slides at this time as you move between frets. When you are ready to move from C to the D chord, *do not lift your hand off the strings*. Rotate your wrist so the bar is lifted a small distance while keeping your damping fingers on the strings, then slide your hand along the strings until you can rotate the bar back to the strings on the seventh fret. After strumming the D chord, again rotate the bar off the strings, quickly lift your left hand off the strings, and strum the G chord. Since you don't yet know the notes on the neck, reference the tab for pitch and use the standard notation for rhythm only at this point.

Track 9
(3:30)

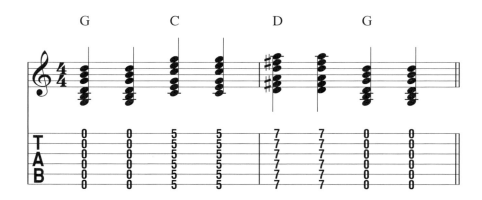

Once the bar is in place for either the C or D chords, make sure that it has firm contact with all six strings. If there is any metallic rattle or a damped string, it indicates that the bar is not on the same plane as the strings. Do not allow the strings to bend downward. On a Dobro, the frets are visual guides, and the strings are never pressed down to the neck—*never!*

Track 10

Let's try a slightly more demanding move with no open-string chords. Again, let's play this *without* slides because this makes you concentrate on accurate bar placement.

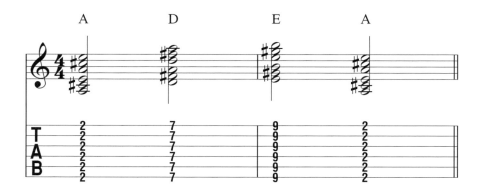

Introducing Grace Notes

Track 11

Another popular technique on the Dobro is the *grace note*. This is a very quick slurred gliss, leading up or down to a note or chord, that's indicated with a small notehead. It occupies no real, measurable time and should be followed immediately with the target note.

Grace notes indicate the pitch at the beginning of a slide. In other words, the notes rhythmic value is subtracted from the principal note. When this technique comes up, listen to the accompanying track and the technique will be obvious.

Let's try our chordal example again with grace-note slides into the D and E chords.

► Beware of the *paralax effect*. Looking at the bar at an angle makes it appear to be lower on the neck than it actually is. It will take only a short time to get used to this and compensate for it without thinking—rely on your ear for this.

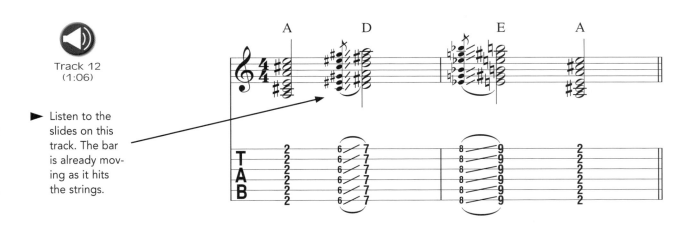

Track 12
(1:06)

► Listen to the slides on this track. The bar is already moving as it hits the strings.

Notes in Open Position

Now that you have a handle on the basic technique, let's learn the names of the notes in open position. Listen to the audio tracks to hear how these notes should sound.

When playing single notes like this on the Dobro, tilt the bar to help minimize bar chatter.

The Sixth String: G

Let's look at the low G string (the sixth string) first. Our first note is G, which is simply the open string.

- The first note, G, is an open-string note. Don't press anything down; just pluck the open sixth string.

On fret 2 of string 6, we have the note A.

- For this note, align the bar over fret 2 of the sixth string, remembering to take into account the parallax effect.

The Fifth String: B

- B is another open-string note. Just pluck the open fifth string.

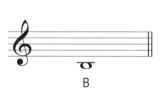

- For the note C, align the bar over fret 1 of the fifth string.

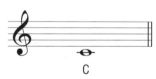

The Fourth String: D

- For the D note, just pluck the fourth string open.

- For the E note, align the bar over fret 2 of the fourth string.

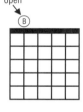

Try playing each of the above notes while saying the note name. Once you're comfortable with that, try playing the following examples. For now, don't add any slides or grace notes. Try to hit each note precisely and in tune.

Track 13

Up and Down

Track 14

Hills and Valleys

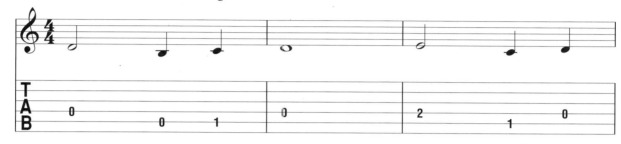

▶ Notice that this is the same pitch as the open fourth string. There are many places to play the same note along the neck of the Dobro.

Let's learn another note on string 5 for the next example.

■ For the D note, align the bar over fret 3 of the fifth string.

In this example, we'll use a quick slide up to the new D note on the fifth string. It doesn't need to be a big one; just slide up from the distance of one fret or so. Listen to the audio to hear how this sounds.

Track 15

Slidin' on Up

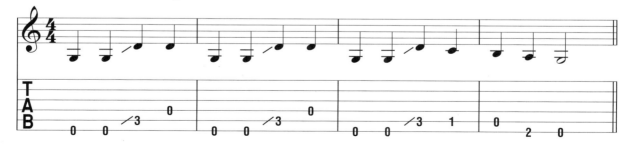

Let's learn some notes on the top strings now.

The Third String: G

- The G note is an open-string note. Don't press anything down; just pluck the open third string.

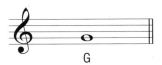

- For the A note, align the bar over fret 2 of the third string.

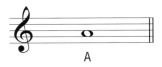

The Second String: B

- For this B note, just pluck the open second string.

- For the note C, align the bar over fret 1 of the second string.

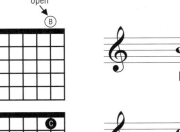

The First String: D

- For the D note, just pluck the first string open.

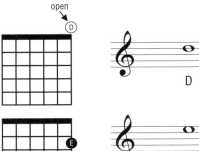

- For the E note, align the bar over fret 2 of the first string.

Staying on the Beat

Having trouble staying on the beat? Try tapping your foot or counting aloud ("1, 2, 3, 4") with each song that you play until you start to develop a natural sense of tempo. Each time you tap your foot will mark one beat.

The ">" symbol in the music indicates when a note is meant to be accented (picked harder than the others). Try to make it a habit of slightly accenting the first note in each measure even if there is no accent mark.

Introducing Rests

While you're usually playing notes in a song, there are times when you play nothing as well. These silences are called **rests**, and they come in different rhythmic values just like notes.

▬	▬	𝄽
Whole Rest (4 beats)	Half Rest (2 beats)	Quarter Rest (1 beat)

When you see a rest, you should quiet your instrument for the specified rhythmic value. This is easily done by touching the strings with your pick hand and/or rotating the bar off the strings and touching them with your barring hand.

Watch out for the rests in these next examples that use the top strings.

Track 16

The Rest Test

Track 17

The Best of the Rest

▶ Notice that this is the same pitch as the open first string. This is the same idea as fret 3 on string 5 matching the open fourth string, only this time it's higher.

Let's learn one more note on string 2.

- For the D note, align the bar over fret 3 of the second string.

For this example, we'll add a quick slide up to the D note on string 2, similarly to the way we did on string 5 in "Slidin' on Up."

 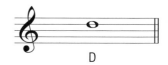

Track 18

Slidin' into Third

Playing Melodies

It's time to play a real tune. I have chosen an easy one so that you can continue concentrating on training your left hand. Before we play it, though, we'll learn another note value.

Introducing Eighth Notes

Thus far, we've dealt with three different rhythmic values: whole notes (four beats), half notes (two beats), and quarter notes (one beat). Now we'll look at the **eighth note**, which lasts for half a beat. It's easy to remember because there are eight eighth notes in a bar of 4/4. They look like a quarter note with a **flag** on the stem. When several appear together, they're connected with a **beam**.

When counting eighth notes, count as you normally would but add "and" in between the counts.

Track 19

Frère Jacques—Melody

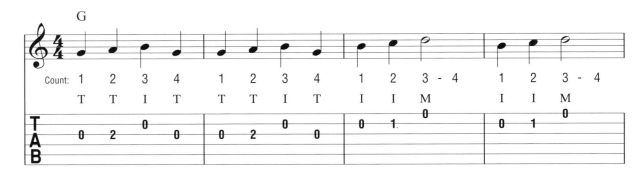

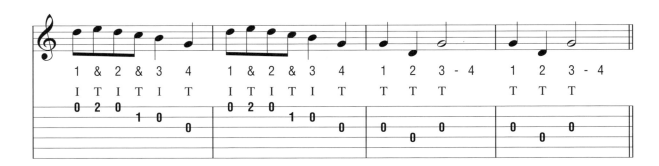

The tempo is slow enough so that any pick-hand fingering will work. My suggestions reflect standard approaches. As a general rule, you can use the middle finger on string 1, index on string 2, and thumb on strings 3–6. But on relatively quick passages, I alternate between the thumb and the index or middle fingers—whichever is more comfortable.

Introducing Octaves

In music, we only use seven different letters in the alphabet. Therefore, we need to recycle them as we move higher or lower in pitch. You'll notice that the open sixth string and the open third string sound the same, only the third string sounds higher. We say that the third string is one **octave** higher than the sixth string. Consequently, you could also say the sixth string is one octave lower than the third string.

Track 21

Let's try the same song one octave down (12 half steps). Since the lower three strings are an octave lower than the top three, the barring is the same, just three strings down. So, what was just played on string 1 should now be played on string 4; string 2 notes are moved to string 5; and string 3 to string 6.

Frère Jacques—Octave Lower

► In the last two measures, we can't go down to the D note as in the original melody because our lowest note is G. Therefore, this D note will be an octave higher than normal.

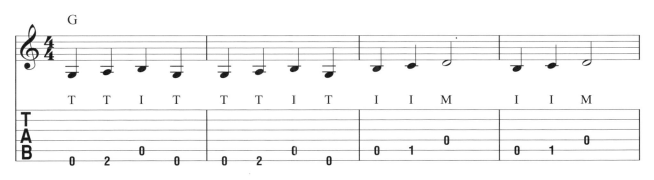

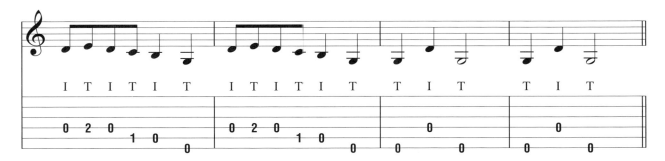

We'll return to "Frère Jacques—Melody" and concentrate on damping. In measures 1 and 2 after picking string 2 open (beat 3, measure 1), get ready to damp. As you pick the next note, string 3 open, the pad of the middle/ring fingers should lightly touch string 2 to stop that string from sounding. At this point, the bar is hovering over the strings, not touching them. Similarly, in measures 5 and 6 after picking the third note, string 1 open, get ready to damp. As you pick string 2 open, the pad of your middle/ring fingers should dampen string 1.

Track 23

Let's try a slightly more demanding arrangement of the same piece. On a Dobro (or any fretted instrument), 12 frets above any note is one octave higher. All the notes have the same names, but the tab will be 12 numbers higher. With this arrangement, there are no open strings, making the barring significantly more demanding. For bar-control practice, avoid slides and keep the bar perpendicular to the frets on each note. This will be challenging when you move from fret 12 to fret 14 and back. You will probably have to twist your wrist a bit to keep the bar straight.

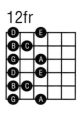

Remember to mute with the middle/ring fingers when the bar moves between strings, as in measures 1–2 and 5–6.

Track 24

Frère Jacques—Octave Higher

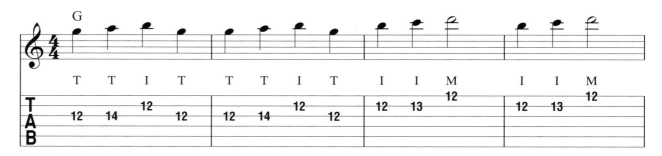

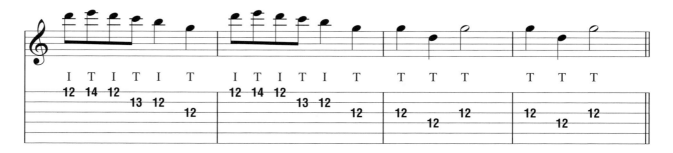

Accidentals

You may have noticed when learning notes on the neck that we skipped some frets. These notes are named with the use of extra symbols called **sharps** or **flats**. These two symbols, along with another called a **natural**, are used to alter the pitch of a note up or down by a **half step** (the distance of one fret on the Dobro). Collectively, these symbols are known as **accidentals**.

A sharp (♯) raises the pitch of a note by one half step.

A flat (♭) lowers the pitch of a note by one half step.

A natural (♮) cancels out a sharp or flat, returning the note to its original pitch.

When the music requires these sharp or flat notes, you'll see the appropriate symbol preceding the note. For this next arrangement of "Frère Jacques," we'll learn two accidentals in the higher octave position: C♯ and F♯.

- For the note C♯, align the bar over fret 11 of the fourth string.

- For the note F♯, align the bar over fret 11 of the third string.

Since we'll be sliding to these notes in "Frère Jacques," practice sliding from D to C♯ and back and then from G to F♯ and back.

Track 25

Sliding and Gliding

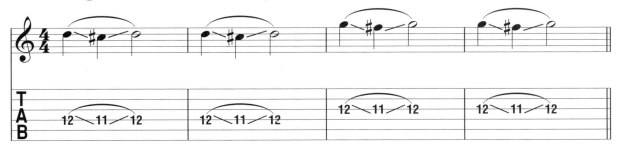

Track 26

This next variation of "Frère Jacques" has the same fretting as the previous one but with the addition of some slides. You don't have to do the same ones that I do, so experiment with other combinations of slurs and attacks.

There is no doubt that it will occasionally be necessary to momentarily grasp the bar, but it is important to teach your hand to return to its default state of maximum relaxation.

Track 27

Frère Jacques—with Slides

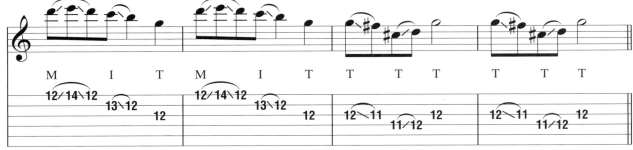

Dots and Ties

When a **dot** is added to a note, it increases its rhythmic value by 50%. So a dotted half note will last three beats instead of two. A dotted quarter note will last one and a half beats instead of one, etc.

| Dotted Half Note (3 beats) | = | Half Note (2 beats) | + | Quarter Note (1 beat) | | Dotted Quarter Note (1 1/2 beats) | = | Quarter Note (1 beat) | + | Eighth Note (1/2 beat) |

A **tie** is a curved line (it looks just like a slur) connecting two notes with the same pitch. When two notes are connected with a tie, their rhythmic values are combined into one continuous note.

count: 1 - 2   3 - 4 - 1   2   3   4 - 1 - 2 - 3   4 - 1 - 2   (3 - 4)

Let's learn two more places to play the note F#: on the fourth and first strings. Remember: these notes are one octave apart.

- For the F# note on string 4, align the bar over fret 4.

- For the F# note on string 1, align the bar over fret 4.

Track 28

All Tied Up

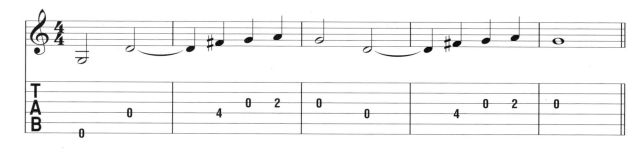

Track 29

Connect the Dots

Track 30

Let's look at one more easy piece before we move on. "Down in the Valley" is a waltz in 3/4 time. In 3/4, there are three beats per bar instead of four. This arrangement has a wider range of pitches, so there's a bit more work to do with the bar.

The last two measures are a **tag**—a sort of musical afterthought. Tags fill the space between the end of a melody and when the next voice or instrument enters. They can vary in length from a couple of beats to a couple of measures, depending on how quickly the next in line jumps in.

Track 31

Down in the Valley—Melody

▶ "N.C." stands for "no chord." In this instance, it's shown because the melody begins before the accompaniment.

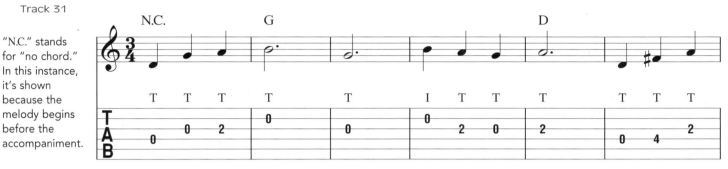

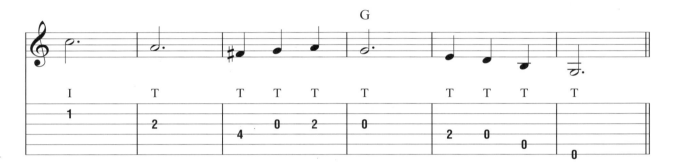

Measures 6–10 may be a little difficult for you at this stage. Try this alternative barring strategy:

Down in the Valley—measures 6–10

Opt for the choice that works best for you or try to find the same notes on yet another string combination. Investigating alternate barring choices should be part of your process of arranging a new tune and *learning the neck* (having the knowledge to find the notes of a melody in any key).

Major Scales and Key Signatures

Track 32

Looking at the Major Scale

If you examine the tablature for examples we've played thus far, you'll notice that the same frets and string combinations keep appearing. This is because both tunes are in the **key** of G major and use the notes of the G major scale. It's worth becoming acquainted with how a G scale looks on our G-tuned Dobro.

Let's look at a G major scale played along one string. As we shall see, all major scales have the same "recipe" of numbers of frets between successive notes (i.e., **intervals**). The notes of the G scale are: G–A–B–C–D–E–F♯–G.

- From G to A is a whole step (two frets)
- From A to B is a whole step
- From B to C is a half step (one fret)
- From C to D is a whole step
- From D to E is a whole step
- From E to F♯ is a whole step
- From F♯ to G is a half step

So, the formula for a major scale is W–W–H–W–W–W–H. To put it in terms of fret numbers between each note, follow the formula: 2–2–1–2–2–2–1.

Play the following to get used to the sound of a major scale and the intervals between the notes. *Try this without any slides.* Hold each note for a whole beat, then mute, and quickly move to the next note. We'll be playing some new notes along the strings here, so cross-reference the tab and/or check the Neck Diagram in the Appendix to learn these.

Here's a G major scale on the third string.

Track 32
(0:36)

And here's the same G major scale on the fourth string. Though the frets are different, *the intervals between the notes are the same.*

Without getting bogged down in jargon, all musicians should know that there are seven different notes (with different letter names) in a major scale. The eighth note has the same letter as the first (here G). The highest- and lowest-pitched notes in this exercise are Gs an octave apart.

Technique Tip!

You may have noticed that it is more difficult to bar accurately when going down the fretboard as opposed to going up, because, in the former, your hand is blocking the view of your fret destination. If there is time, I try to glimpse that fret even as the previous note is still sounding—that way, I have an idea of the next move in advance.

It turns out to be easier to play cleanly (i.e., accurately and without slides) at quick tempos if we play *across* the strings instead of *along* one string. Try these variations of the G major scale. Notice how "Frère Jacques" uses Exercises A and B:

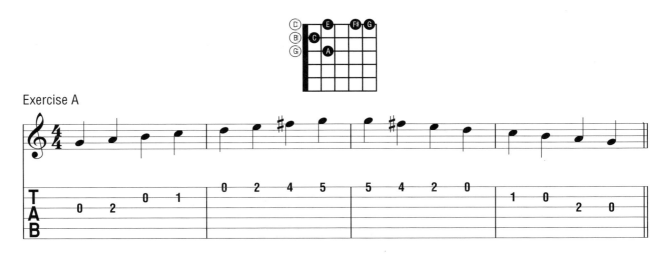

Exercise A

Exercise B

Exercise C

Track 33

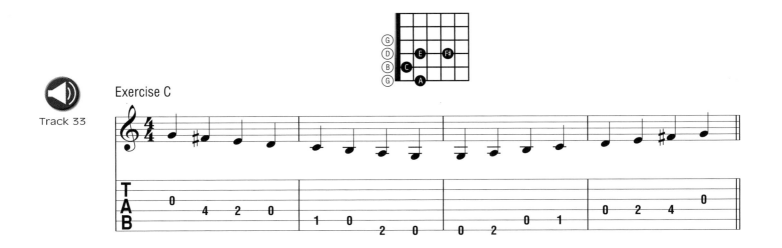

The next two versions of the scale (Exercises D and E) are especially useful because the patterns can easily be shifted up or down the neck to get major scales in other keys (in music jargon, *transposed*).

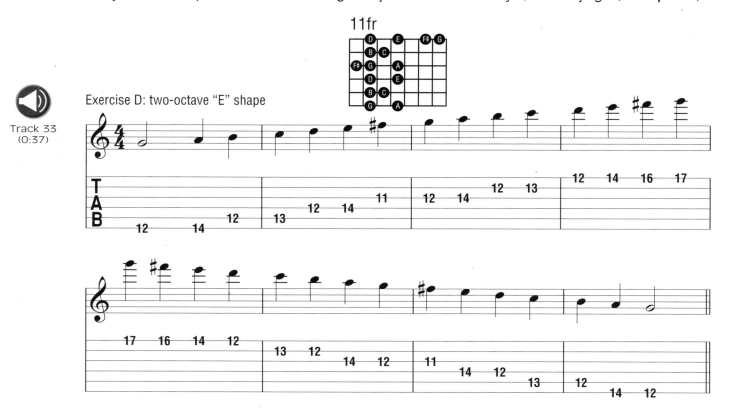

Exercise D: two-octave "E" shape

I have found it particularly useful to think of the pattern's overall shape. Just looking at only the notes of Exercise D on the top three strings, the pattern looks like the letter "E."

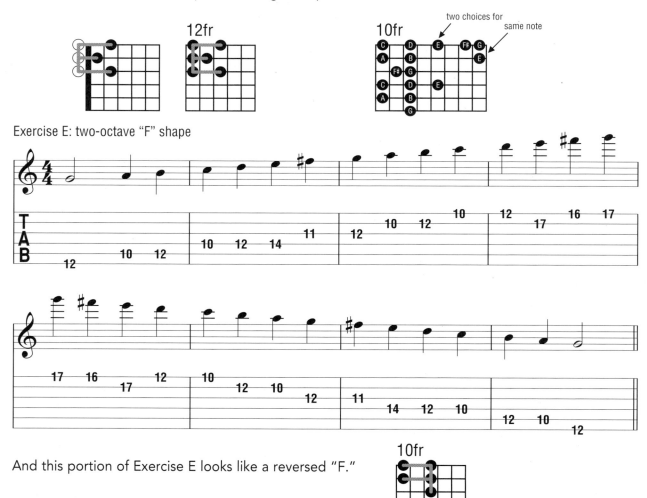

two choices for same note

Exercise E: two-octave "F" shape

And this portion of Exercise E looks like a reversed "F."

Why only five or six notes? You'll find that that portion of a scale forms a comfortable "pocket" where you can often play for several measures at a time, or even entire tunes, with minimal hand movement (i.e., economy of motion).

Don't try to memorize these patterns right now. You'll learn by repetition in the tunes that follow. Eventually, you'll visualize the scale shapes when you look at the strings.

Key Signatures

Every major scale (there are 12 different ones) uses a different set of notes. We've only been using natural and sharp notes so far, but some scales use flat notes as well. The G major scale, for example, contains one sharp: F♯. But if we want to build a D major scale, for example, we have to use F♯ and C♯.

Since music is written in different keys and therefore uses mostly the same sets of notes in one piece, we use **key signatures** to avoid writing the same sharps or flats over and over. The key signature is a collection of sharps or flats at the beginning of the staff telling the performer what key the song is in.

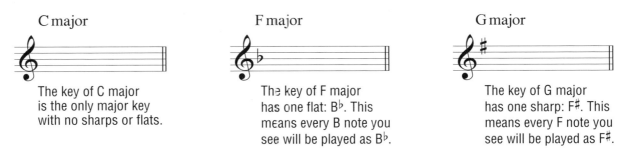

C major	F major	G major
The key of C major is the only major key with no sharps or flats.	The key of F major has one flat: B♭. This means every B note you see will be played as B♭.	The key of G major has one sharp: F♯. This means every F note you see will be played as F♯.

For reference, you can find all 12 key signatures in the Appendix.

Let's learn a new note, F, to play in the key of C major.

- For the note F, align the bar with fret 3 on string 1 (high octave) or string 4 (low octave).

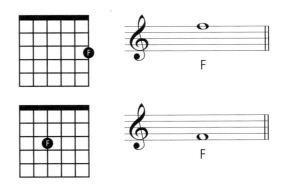

Track 34

Key of C

Key of G

Track 35

► Remember!
The key signa-
ture tells you
to play all the
F notes as F#!

Track 36

Let's try a tune in the key of D major and get familiar with the scale. Note that the key of D major has two sharps: F# and C#. To start, we'll play the D major scale all on string 3 as a reminder that all major scales have the same interval structure. Then we'll look at the same D scale with the first six notes using the E-shape pattern. Note that the latter is the same pattern as the G scale that began on fret 12, just shifted down five frets.

D major scale on 1 string

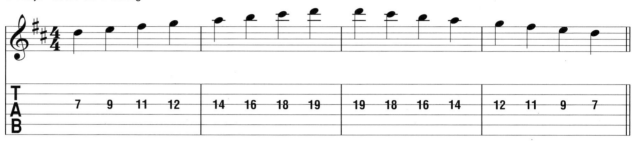

D major scale shape

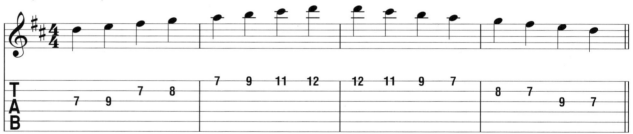

Pickup Notes

The following song, "Sailor on the Deep Blue Sea," begins with what's called a *pickup measure*. This is an incomplete measure at the beginning of a piece of music that's used when the melody begins before the song's accompaniment. In this case, there are two beats of pickup notes (two quarter notes), so you would count "1, 2," then play the two pickup notes ("3, 4") to lead the song in.

Note that the pickup measure is not counted in the measure numbering for a song.

Here's a tune made famous by the Carter Family in the 1930s, as well as Flatt & Scruggs and the New Lost City Ramblers in the 1960s. The lyrics are supplied for reference.

Track 37

Sailor on the Deep Blue Sea

▶ Note that we're playing the B note in measures 3–4 and 11–12 at fret 12, string 2 instead of fret 9, string 1. This is simply to facilitate the sliding maneuver.

Track 38

Since this song is in the key of D, and a D chord is located at the seventh fret, the playing is centered there.

In measure 3, start the slide around fret 11, slide quickly, and end spot-on fret 12. You can place the bar flat as you slide and let the pitch on string 2, fret 12 ring as string 1 is picked. This sounds harmonious because both notes are part of the G chord's underlying harmony.

So Many Notes, So Many Positions

So how do you decide which variation of the scale pattern to use? Sometimes it's the way a particular melody is shaped, but as is often the case, it's a personal choice as to which is easier for the individual player.

For example, in measure 13 of "Sailor on the Deep Blue Sea," the shape of the melody dictates my choice. I find the following alternative more difficult to play in tune, unless you want to slide through all the notes—not my favorite sound.

These are the sort of choices you should consider when you start to create your own arrangements. As you are discovering, there is no reason to use only one pattern on any particular song or lick. Use what is easier for you.

31

Here is a song in the key of A that allows a combination of closed and open strings. The key of A major has three sharps: F♯, C♯, and G♯. The open-string options make the F-shape pattern the easiest. Over the years, "Jimmie Brown, the Newsboy" has been prominent in the repertoires of Flatt & Scruggs, Mac Wiseman, the Carter Family, and Bill Monroe.

Here's the scale form from which we're working here. Note that the G♯ note at fret 1 on the third string is new.

We're also sliding down a half step (one fret) from E at fret 2, string 4 to an E♭ note at fret 1. This is the first time we've seen a flat note. Moving from a natural note down a half step makes that note flat (i.e., E to E♭).

Track 39

Jimmie Brown, the Newsboy

I advise damping string 2 and string 3, before the slide that begins measure 2, to avoid dissonance. The open strings are part of the F-shape pattern, while the string 1, fret 4 note may be considered part of the E-shape pattern. The notes of measure 8 are another tag; decide which parts you wish to play with a tilted or flat bar.

Time to check your technique:

- Lay the bar across the lowest five strings at the second fret, leaving string 1 open.

- Play string 2, don't block, then open string 1.

- Now slide the bar across the strings to play string 1 at fret 2.

- Full marks if the bar doesn't "catch" on the first string. If it does, it indicates that you are pressing down on the bar!

Chord Accompaniment

Track 40

Odds are that you are also interested in using your instrument to accompany yourself and/or friends at jam sessions. Let's explore some things you need to know to play solid rhythmic support.

The basic right-hand strum for standard guitar also works well for Dobro players. It consists of a plucked bass note (i.e., low strings) followed by a strum of anywhere from three to six strings. For country, bluegrass, and folk rhythms, each attack is usually a quarter note in duration, and the pattern is known as a "boom-chick" or "oom-pah" rhythm.

For example, on "Frère Jacques," the accompaniment is all G chords. The strum can be picked with just the thumb, just the index and/or middle fingers, or in a pinching motion using all three fingers.

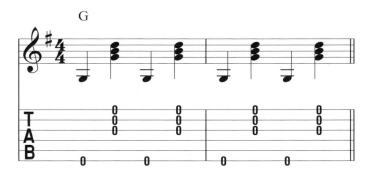

Track 41

A little more interesting, and the choice of most country and bluegrass guitarists, is the **alternating bass** technique, where the plucked bass note alternates between the sixth and fourth strings.

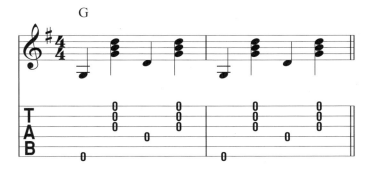

It will take a bit of time for your thumb to get used to moving between the sixth and fourth strings without hitting the fifth string by mistake. Practice it as slow as necessary to achieve consistency. Don't worry if it is stupidly slow at first. Do it too fast, and you will just be repeatedly practicing mistakes.

Do not get in the habit of looking at your picking hand. It is more critical to make sure that the bar is in the right spot. With practice, you might be able to look up from the Dobro and flirt with someone across the room. Then you will be stepping up to the next level of proficiency.

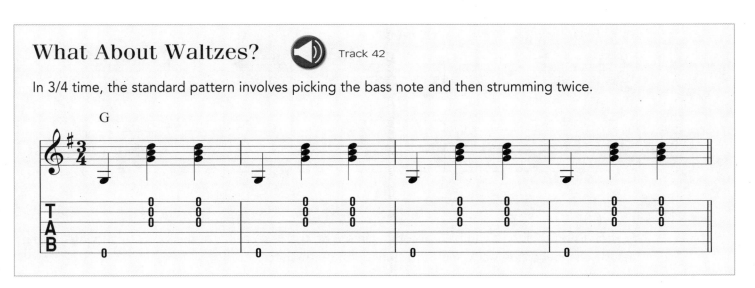

What About Waltzes?   Track 42

In 3/4 time, the standard pattern involves picking the bass note and then strumming twice.

"Sailor on the Deep Blue Sea" from Lesson 6 has a typical three-chord *progression*. Also, no slides, please. That's not easy at this stage of learning to control the bar. When the chords change, just move the bar to the correct fret. (See the Appendix for a diagram of where to find the major chords.)

Sailor on the Deep Blue Sea— Accompaniment

You can listen to alternating bass accompaniment on the other tunes in this book by turning off the melody channel of the track and just listening to the rhythm.

Introducing Staccato

On bluegrass tunes, a technique called "chunking" (or "chopping") is typically played on Dobro. This is a short, sharp strum usually played with a pinching motion by the thumb and index and/or middle fingers. The musical term for playing notes in a short, clipped manner is **staccato**, indicated by a dot above (or below) the notehead.

Try this example to get a feel for the staccato technique. You can stop a fretted note by simply rotating the bar slightly off the strings and touching them with your damping fingers. Alternatively, you can bring your pick-hand palm down onto the strings. When damping open strings, the latter method usually works best.

Short and to the Point

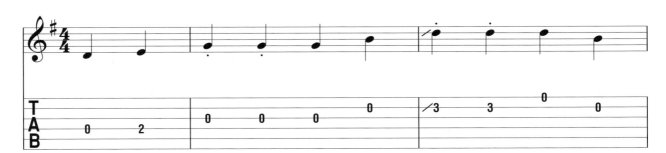

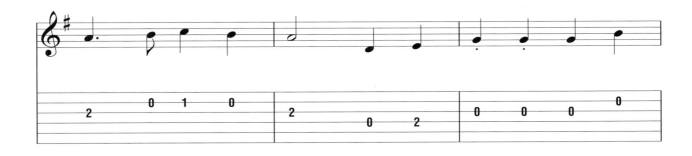

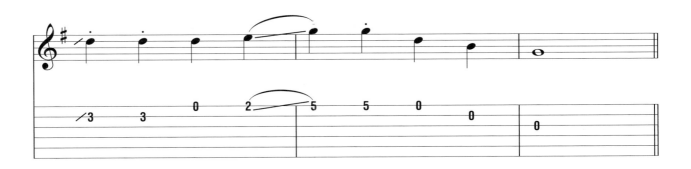

On "Sailor on the Deep Blue Sea," the G chord is chunked at fret 12 (instead of open) because it is easier to damp fretted strings (just picking up the bar slightly) than open strings (bringing your palm down onto the strings). Let's give it a try:

Track 46

Sailor on the Deep Blue Sea—Chops

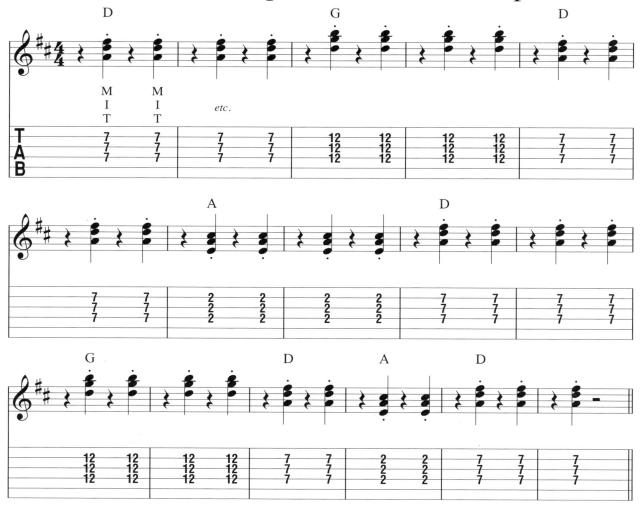

Some players like to have some metallic rattle in their chunks, which makes them sound a bit like a hi-hat cymbal in the kit of a drummer. Others almost completely block the strings, creating a sort of "thunk." Experiment with how firmly the bar touches the strings when chunking and, of course, listen to your favorite players.

Depending on the style of music, there are other right-hand picking patterns that can be used for accompaniment, but that will have to wait for your next instruction book.

Time to check your technique:

- Are both hands relaxed? If either wrist feels achy, give it a rest.
- Are your ring and middle fingers available for blocking? Is there any bar chatter?
- Are you playing in time?
- Are you experimenting with playing while standing?
- Are you looking at your picking hand while playing? Your eyes need to be on the bar to guarantee accuracy!

Double Stops & Vibrato

Double Stops

Track 47

Let's add some spice to our playing. One of the most pleasing of the easy techniques everyone uses on Dobro is **double stops**. This refers to playing two strings simultaneously so there is a harmony along with the melody. To bar on more than one string at a time, the bar has to be flat (not tilted).

This approach fits well in a tune we've already looked at: "Down in the Valley." Instead of using open strings, we'll move up an octave so all the notes are fretted. Why? It's time to add vibrato! Just listen to the track for now to hear how the vibrato (indicated by the wavy, horizontal lines) sounds. You'll soon learn how to create it. Reference the tab for note positions here.

Track 48

Down in the Valley—with Double Stops and Vibrato

► Remember that the grace notes (small notes with a slash through the stem) that precede certain notes receive no real rhythmic value. The bar is already moving when it hits the strings in these instances, creating a smear of pitch before reaching the destination note.

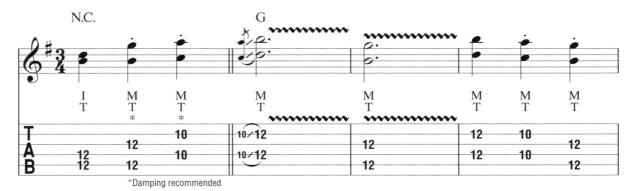

*Damping recommended

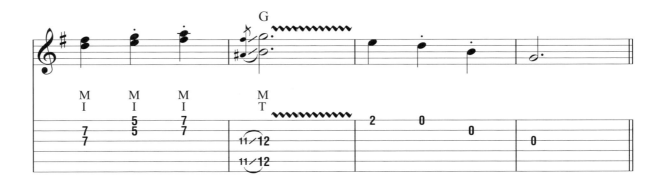

In this setting, the melody is the upper (higher-pitched) note, and the harmony is the lower note of each double stop. As a teaching tool, I have harmonized every note. When performing, I would ordinarily play a mix of single notes and double stops, seasoned to my taste at the moment.

With double stops, damping (or blocking) becomes more critical—not only to avoid bar chatter, but because there are also some sour notes that are not part of the scale (here G major) or underlying chords. (The "*" indicate where damping is highly recommended.) The sound of two strings sliding can detract from the melody, and measure 6 can be frightening if you don't damp. Refer back to tracks 9 and 22 if you need more practice with damping. Listen to the previous double-stop version of "Down in the Valley" played on Track 49 without damping. Be forewarned; it's not pretty!

Vibrato

Vibrato is a smooth, back-and-forth oscillation of the bar usually done while a note is held. This technique can add some sustain and a bit of warmth and emotion to your playing. In most cases, the motion is less than a fret in width. Simple as this skill may seem, it takes much patience to develop smoothness and consistency of motion.

All motion should be from the wrist to the fingers. The exact speed and distance is an individual choice and dependent on the style of music being played. In folk, country, and bluegrass, the general approach is to let the pitch ring for a moment, note duration allowing, then begin the vibrato, gradually increasing the frequency and width as the sound decays. Listen to the track for the sound of vibrato with a tilted bar on string 1, fret 5.

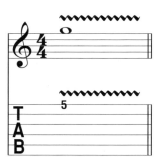

Some Dobro players like to keep bar motion no higher in pitch than the target fret (here fret 5). Others like to center the motion around that fret (i.e., equally above and below that point).

On "Down in the Valley," try vibrato on all the notes that are held for three beats. On notes of shorter duration, there usually isn't enough time for it to be effective. Go back to Track 48 and listen again to hear vibrato used on the version with double stops (pg. 37).

Next is "Down in the Valley (Melody)—with Vibrato" with some of the open-string notes replaced with barred ones to allow vibrato. (These replacements have been indicated with an asterisk.) There is more character to the music with vibrato, even with this basic version.

You might find it a bit easier to vibrato the C note at string 3, fret 5 because there is more room to oscillate the bar.

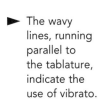

Track 51

Down in the Valley (Melody)—with Vibrato

► The wavy lines, running parallel to the tablature, indicate the use of vibrato.

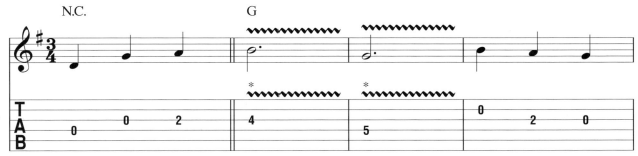

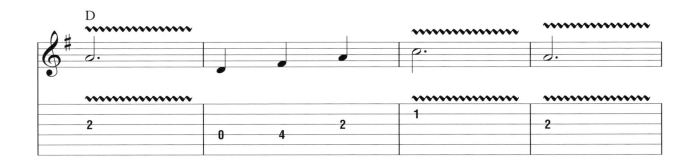

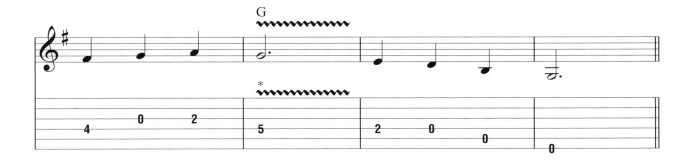

Track 52

"Sailor on the Deep Blue Sea" can also benefit from some vibrato (see pg. 31). There are no open strings, so everything could be fodder for vibrato. Here's how it sounds with vibrato added to the longer, sustained notes.

Time to check your technique:

- Are your hands relaxed?
- Is there any bar chatter?
- Are you playing in time?
- Are your eyes on the bar (where they should be)?
- Are you strumming the chords to the tunes that you are learning?
- Are you sliding every time you move the bar? Don't overuse that effect. Make your playing a mix of slides and non-slides.

Lesson 9 | Rolls

Any Dobro player interested in bluegrass music needs to know something about **three-finger rolls**. Their importance is often overstressed; they are only of use in a minority of tunes, but those are the fast barn-burners!

But even the fastest tunes must be learned slowly at first. Work up the next piece even stupidly slowly, and you'll have it. If you cut corners and play the rolls sloppily, you will learn the sloppy way really well and have all sorts of trouble unlearning the mistakes.

Rolls on the Dobro are based on the way Buck "Uncle Josh" Graves applied the three-finger style made famous by the great banjo innovator, Earl Scruggs, back in the '50s, so there is a whole lot of "banjo-ness" to this technique. In keeping with this idea, it is okay to not mute each note and let the notes overlap.

The concept of the forward roll is quite simple. Play consecutive eighth notes on different strings in this order: thumb, index, middle. Here are two consecutive rolls using open strings.

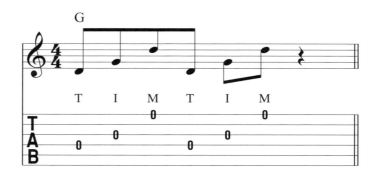

Let's avoid a beginner's misconception right off the bat: These are played as eighth notes—*not* eighth-note triplets.

Repeat Signs and Numbered Endings

Repeat signs are double-bar lines with two dots (see music for "Long Journey Home [Two Dollar Bill]"), and they indicate that you play the music in between them twice. The brackets above the music indicate that you play the music under the **first ending** the first time; the second time, you skip the first ending and jump to the **second ending**.

We'll use the bluegrass standard, "Long Journey Home (Two Dollar Bill)" to get 'er rolling. To see how we fit it into the roll pattern, here is the basic melody.

Track 54

Long Journey Home (Two Dollar Bill)— Melody

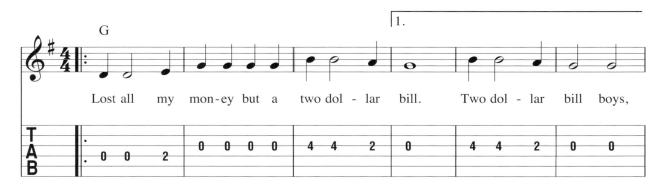

Lost all my mon-ey but a two dol - lar bill. Two dol - lar bill boys,

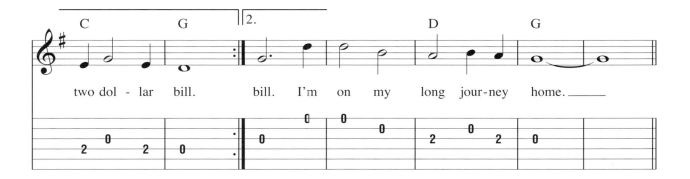

two dol - lar bill. bill. I'm on my long jour-ney home. _____

That's kind of plain sounding. The three-finger roll changes all that.

Track 55

Typically, there are a lot fewer notes to the melody than in instrumentals. Banjo-type rolls fill the measure with a ton of musical energy. The trick is to highlight the melody notes amidst all of that sound.

To minimize what you have to think about, the next arrangement employs the same pattern in every measure (until the very end): what I call the "3–3–2 pattern." Instead of one continuous roll through-out the piece, play two of them, then two notes of a third, and then begin anew in the next measure. The idea is to make the roll fit into one measure (since only eight eighth notes fit). This approach helps you keep track of where you are in the song, and since there always is a new roll on the first beat of each measure, it ensures that your thumb (the strongest finger) is ready for that note.

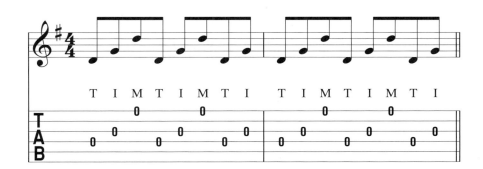

Why this choice of "gapped" strings (i.e., omitting string 2)? These rolls exclude the open string 2 because it's the one most difficult to keep in tune. In rolls, we tend to minimize that particular open string (though not eliminate it), which can muddy the sound.

Notice that, typical of old bluegrass repertoire, many measures have an important note on beat 4 and another on beat 1 of the next measure. The 3–3–2 pattern enables your strongest finger to play both of these notes. By comparing the original melody to the next arrangement, you will see that melody notes often occur in rolls at the exact same beat as the basic melody.

Track 56

Long Journey Home (Two Dollar Bill)— with Three-Finger Rolls

► The natural sign (♮) on the note F at the second ending tells you to ignore the key signature (which specifies F#) temporarily and play F instead. The B♭ note at fret 3 on string 3 is a new one and provides a bluesy sound (as does the F♮) in the key of G.

Track 57

Listen to the track a couple times before practicing. It will help the learning process if you already have the sound that you are striving for in your brain. There are lots of repeated, overlapping pitches here for that banjo sound.

That B note on string 4, fret 9 is the same pitch as string 3, fret 4 in the basic melody of "Long Journey Home." Likewise, in measure 7, string 5, fret 5 is the same pitch (E) as string 4, fret 2 in measure 7 of the basic melody.

Sometimes the basic melody notes sync up perfectly with the roll. Other times they are displaced by an eighth note. In context, and with some thought, a tasty mixture of on-the-beat and syncopated melody is created. *Syncopation* is the placement of accents on weak beats, such as the "and" when counting eighth notes.

Notice how the slides are used to help accent certain notes. Accents on unexpected parts of the measure add syncopation to rolls.

Even three-finger rolls can get tiresome, so I inserted a blues-type riff for a hot ending. You can hear (and see in the notation) that there are some notes that are not part of the G major scale. Oversimplifying a bit, these are the third and seventh notes of the scale played one fret lower (flatted). When flatted, these notes are often referred to as blue notes.

Track 58

Here are two variations that will give you ideas for getting away from one roll pattern for an entire solo. The first is a fretting substitution for measures 3 and 4—almost the same notes.

Alternate rolls for measures 3–4

The next are two variants of the 3–3–2 pattern: 2–3–3 and 3–2–3 patterns. Tossing in an occasional roll variant makes for added syncopation and more exciting listening. Measures 1–2 are used to illustrate these rolls, but they could fit in any measure.

Alternate rolls for measures 1–2

2–3–3 Roll

3–2–3 Roll

There are other variations—reverse (M–I–T), forward-reverse (T–I–M–I–T), and others without names—but this introduction will get you well underway.

Time to check your technique:

- Are you playing slowly enough to get the timing right?
- Are both hands relaxed?
- Are you experimenting with picking at various distances from the bridge?
- Is there any bar chatter?

Hammer-Ons & Pull-Offs

When playing medium and up-tempo tunes in the key of G, *hammer-ons* and *pull-offs* are a necessity for your savings bank account of Dobro techniques. (They are used in other keys but are especially handy in the key of G). These techniques decrease the need for picking and can make fast playing easier (especially when you are a rookie).

Track 59

Hammer-Ons

To hammer-on, first pick the open fourth string, letting it ring for an eighth-note duration. Now bring the tilted tip of the bar straight down with some force onto the second fret. If you just lay the bar gently onto the string, the volume of the hammered note will be relatively quiet. The hammer-on force is an important part of this technique. This technique is indicated in the notation with a slur to a higher pitch.

Hammer-ons are an exception to the rule that your damping fingers should precede the bar onto the strings. (If the damping fingers do precede the bar, the string will be muted, and the hammered note will be very quiet.) To minimize bar chatter, however, damping fingers should touch the hammered string almost simultaneously with the bar.

Track 60

Hammering Away

Track 61

Hammering It Home

► In this example, we use a hammer-on followed immediately by a slurred gliss (slide) several times (measures 1 and 2–3). In these instances, you should pick only once to sound all three notes.

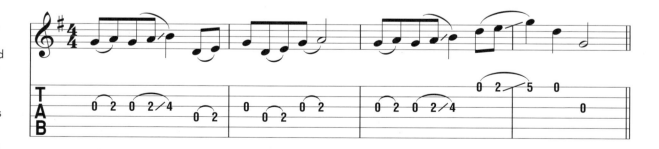

44

Pull-Offs

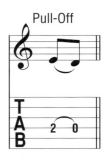

Pull-Off

To perform a pull-off, pick string 4, fret 2 with a tilted bar and slightly depress the string. (This is an exception to our rule to not press down on strings.) Pull the bar across (perpendicular to) the string toward string 5. Since the tip (not the middle) of the bar is touching string 4, that should be a very short distance. String 4 should pop off the tip and vibrate, sounding the pitch of the open D string. The bar should then be silently resting on string 5.

Remember to slightly lift your damping fingers off the string when pulling off so the open string will be allowed to vibrate.

Can You Pull This One Off?

Don't Pull My Leg

▶ Remember the key signature! This song is in the key of D major, so every F and C note is sharped.

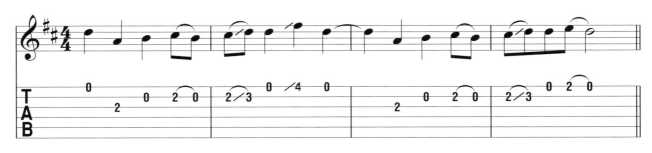

"Hot Corn, Cold Corn" is a bluegrass classic that features both hammer-ons and pull-offs. This is not just the melody. There are a few licks and extra notes to add to the fun. As usual, take it *slow*.

Pick hard on this piece—that is the bluegrass way. Bluegrass bands have loud banjos and guitars whose pitch range is about the same as a Dobro, so we have to get used to making an effort to be heard in jam sessions.

The slides in measures 1, 5, and 9 should be accented. Pick even harder! Those slides should be fast and about one fret in length.

Listen for the combination of damping some notes and letting others ring on the recording. Try to block all the second-fret notes (after letting them sound for their full duration) in this piece. This is not a general rule; it is just the way it works in this arrangement.

Don't be intimidated by the change of time signature towards the end of the song. Listen to the track, and it will make perfect sense without bothering to count. If you do count, all the measures have four beats except the one in 2/4; count two beats and then move on to the next measure 4/4.

Hey guys, you're playing the real deal!

Hot Corn, Cold Corn

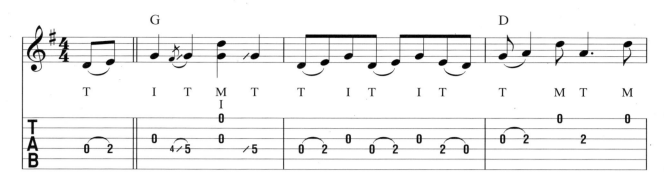

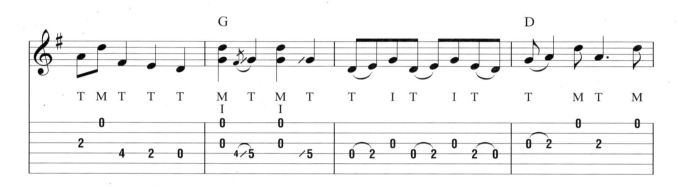

Final Technique Check:

- Listen carefully to your playing to make sure that mistakes are not creeping in. Make a recording of your playing and evaluate it.

- If you can't seem to play a particular phrase without mistakes, make sure that fingering is not the problem. Are you trying to play two consecutive eighth notes with the same pick-hand finger?

- Are your middle and ring fingers available for blocking?

- Are you playing in time? Try playing with just the rhythm channel of the accompanying audio recording. Buy a **metronome** (electronic time-keeper available at any music store)!

- Don't look at your pick hand while playing.

- Are you overusing slides?

- Are you adding occasional vibrato to notes of longer duration?

Lesson 11 Next Steps

If you have played through the whole book, I am confident that you are now ready to shine at the next jam session and start creating your own adaptations. Don't hesitate to change the ones in this book. You can omit or add notes, change a hammer-on to a picked note, add or delete slides, alter the speed and length of those slides—the possibilities are endless. Just make sure that any changes still fit the meter and chords.

When you practice by yourself, don't fall into the trap of playing fast on the easy parts and slowing down on the challenging sections. Use a metronome to ensure that your rhythm is steady. Playing along with your favorite recordings will also make you aware of timing.

For the next phases of your instruction, consider my other instructional guides. They will lead you to more advanced applications of rolls, hammer-ons, and pull-offs, as well as new techniques like slants, harmonics, and string bends.

The Dobro Book:

The next step after this book, long considered the best teaching text for Dobro.

Dobro Techniques and Repertoire:

Two DVDs for the intermediate player, concentrating on how to create your own solos.

Visit my website for more information at **www.stacyphillips.com**.

Appendix

Neck Diagram of Notes

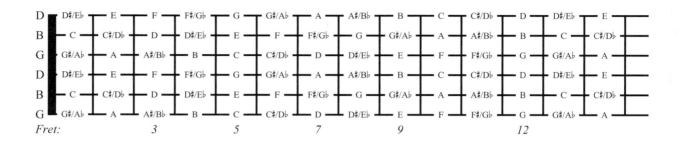

Major Chord Finder

Barring across the strings produces the following major chords:

Fret:	0	1	2	3	4	5	6	7	8	9	10	11	12
Major Chord:	G	G♯/A♭	A	A♯/B♭	B	C	C♯/B♭	D	D♯/E♭	E	F	F♯/G♭	G

Major Key Signatures

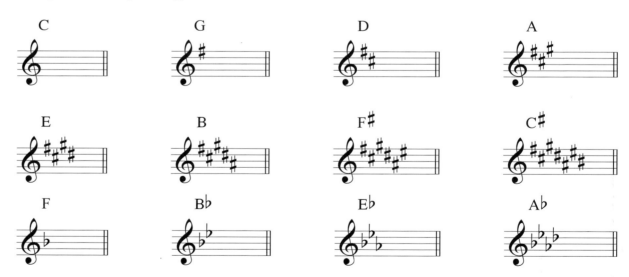